Welcome to you,
to our class Christmas play.
My name is Sam –
          your narrator today.

And I'm playing Mary –
the star of the show!
Everyone comfortable?
Ready? Let's go!

I stroll on the stage
past the tall Christmas tree,
the whole room of parents
all looking at ME...

Hey! Who put that there?
Right there in the way!
Why's there a tent in
my class Christmas play?

Ladies and Gentlemen, that Christmas time
the high King of heaven left riches behind,
and like God was camping, with no pride or fuss,
he came down from heaven
and lived among us.

This is my **BIG** scene – just Angel and me.
Fear and surprise! I'm a new mum-to-be.
But wait! There's no way Mary had that at home.
So why has the playscript included a phone?

No matter the distance, whatever the place,
with video calls we can chat face to face.
We might think of Jesus a bit like a phone –
showing us God and so making him known.

Signpost? Check! Luggage? Check!
We're on our way.
Let's nail the travelling scene of the play.
Riding to Bethlehem on a... Wait! What?
Who thought a lion was part of the plot?

BETHLEHM

When you see a lion you think of one thing:
strength, might, his power –
            he's called "Jungle **KING**".
So don't think of Jesus as just weak and small.
        He's King of the universe – he rules it all.

Our journey is over. Next scene is a win.
Say it together: "No room at the inn!"
Oh no! Why's the audience starting to laugh?
Since when did the innkeeper have extra staff?

The more you have power – it's generally true –
the more you get others to do things for you.
But not so King Jesus. He made and rules earth,
yet just like that waiter he offers to serve.

The famous birth scene with the spotlight on me.
And Joseph... And baby too... Just us three.
So, what is **SHE** doing? Did she not rehearse?
Everyone knows that this scene has no nurse!

Don't be surprised. Yes, a nurse does belong.
She helps and she heals since she knows what is wrong.
Well, so too with Jesus, who came to fix sin –
the ways that we choose not to treat God as King.

I exit the stage now for shepherds and sheep.
But look through the curtain — we'll still take a peep.
Tea towels as headdresses, each has a crook.
Hang on! That's a mop that she's holding there! Look!

The effect of our sin's like a stain we can't see,
and can't be scrubbed out — not by you, not by me.
So Jesus was born to do what we **CAN'T** do:
to clean up our hearts and to make them brand new.

Now it's the big scene with actors galore:
dozens of angels out there on the floor!
But this scene does not involve having to float,
so why's my nativity boasting a boat?

If we know we're in danger, "Please save me!" we shout.
Then we trust in the person whose arms lift us out.
Like a lifeboat that races to you through the waves,
here's our Rescuer, Jesus! He seeks and he saves.

I'm back in the stable, but this is all wrong.
It should be the wise men who bring gifts along.
So what's there to learn then? Since clearly tonight
there's more to all this than there seems at first sight.

The best gift you'll get has no wrapping or tag.
It's not from a shop and won't fit in a bag.
The best gift is Jesus, who says, "Be my friend.
And let me invite you to life without end."

I used to think I was the star – me alone.
I never once asked why the manger's a throne.
But now I can see that it's just the right thing.
I'm not the star – it's the Rescuing King.

Let's clap all the actors as they take their bow.

The **NURSE** with the **WAITER**, the **LION** standing proud.

TENT, PHONE, THRONE, BOAT, MOP, GIFT out on the floor...

So now, can you tell me:
What were they all for?

JESUS IS...

God living
among us,

John 1 v 14

the way God shows
himself to us,

John 1 v 18

and the powerful
Creator King.

Isaiah 9 v 6

JESUS CAME...

to serve,

Mark 10 v 45

to fix the problem
of sin,

Mark 2 v 17

to do what
we can't,

Ezekiel 36 v 25-27

to rescue us,

Luke 19 v 10

and to offer us an
amazing gift.

Romans 6 v 23

Jesus should be centre-stage
at Christmas — and all year!

Philippians 2 v 8-11